CHII

Controlling anger

The Rogue Hypnotist

Disclaimer: this book is not intended as a replacement for skilled, qualified and appropriate 'therapy' by a skilled practitioner. It is for your educational and entertainment purposes only.

At times the words may seem 'funny', 'ungrammatical' etc. - this is 100% intentional, for this is a book directed to both minds.

We are in tough times; I am producing a series of affordable books to help people deal more effectively with times of crisis, change, or transition. When you genuinely do feel more in control - handling change is far easier...

The Rogue Hypnotist Collection.

The Confessions Of series:

How to Hypnotise Anyone

Mastering Hypnotic Language

Powerful Hypnosis.

Forbidden Hypnotic Secrets

Wizards of Trance

Crafting Hypnotic Spells

Escaping Cultural Hypnosis

Hypnotically Deprogramming Addiction

Hypnotically Annihilating Anxiety

Weirdnosis.

The Force of Suggestion series:

The Force of Suggestion: Foundations

Changing Perceptions

Trojan Horses

The Persuasion Force Series:

Persuasion Force Volume 1: Everyday Psi-Ops

Alchemical Persuasion

Invasion of the Mind

The How to Manipulate Everyone Series:

How to Manipulate Everyone: Exposing the MindBenders

Defend Your Mind

Take Back Control

The How to Block Brainwashing series:

How to Block Brainwashing: The Soul Stealers

Downloading Delusions

Selling Hell

Self Help that Works series:

The Confidence Book: How to Stay Sane in a World Gone Mad

How to Solve Any Problem: Meta-Strategies for Life

Make Happiness Happen

The Rogue Hypnotist Investigates Series (folklore/occult):

Wicked Teeth: The Secret History of Werewolves

Seductive Blood: The Horrific History of Vampires

INTRO: A BOOK ON ANGER!

Word origins. From the Old Norse *angra* - to be vexed; to take offence. There was the Old English *enge* - narrow, painful. It was ultimately derived from the Proto-Indo-European word *angh* - tight, painfully constricted, painful. In both Greek and Latin its variants referred to strangling.

What is causing that pain that leads to a narrow focus that makes you want to attack? That is what we will uncover in this book. **The real source of all anger is <u>frustration</u>.** A word linked to the idea of being deceived. Disappointment, defeat. Angry people often do feel cheated in some way. But if we are 'cheated' what is the best way to respond?

Anger arises when our efforts do not work. It also arises when we take 'offence' (originally meaning against killing) at an 'insult': a word derived from the PIE *en-salire*: to leap upon - to be attacked. Actually an attack within. An attack on us. The question is - what is the best way to respond to an 'attack'? I bet no one is trying to kill you, so...

Do you feel frustrated about something? What is it specifically?

Do you feel disappointed about something? What specifically?

Has someone insulted you? Were they rude? Why did it cause you such offence that it became 'painful'?

If someone attacks you you can respond in a variety of ways. In a way getting angry shows you have standards. Most people are crushed by an attack. They often run away like cowards. An 'angry person' turns on the 'attack'/'attacker' and fights back. That shows a level of self-respect.

Anger has its uses: the purpose of this book is NOT to remove anger. In some circumstances anger is fully understandable, and it can get results. However, it is only one tool. Wouldn't you rather have a bigger bag of more effective tools that got better results? Of course. And that is why you're here.

The word rude literally meant red. Probably derived from the legendary rudeness of the red-haired Scythians. PIE - *reudh* - red. It is time to control how often you see red, no matter what the provocations are. If someone successfully provokes you they have control over you.

There is nothing wrong with aggression - PIE *ad* - near/at + PIE *ghredh* - grade, to walk, go, step. To pursue with energy. There is nothing wrong with being determined or driven. Driven people succeed. The problem with anger, with uncontrolled aggression, is that it can backfire on you; leading to more anger and more uncontrolled aggression. You have got trapped in a 'reactionary' anger loop.

I am guessing you are here because you want to stop being so angry. You came to the right place. Do you sometimes experience rages? This meant madness, rabies: PIE *rebh* - violent, impetuous. Hot-tempered. Bad-tempered. I am guessing you would like to *be good-tempered* more often? I don't blame you. Anger, in excess, is draining. Not much fun. I've never met a really angry baby. This means that somewhere on your life's journey you learnt to be angry. That's good news. If you learnt that, you can learn to CHILL. You can learn to control all that energy and save it for getting your real needs met. Then you'll be more successful - in the widest sense. Far less frustrated. Less pained. Sound like a deal?

The Rageometre!

Let's objectively rate your anger. I call this section the rageometre for good reason. There is evidence that when we rate an emotion numerically we immediately calm down a bit. Why? Anger, like fear, shuts down the thinking mind. Your 'higher mind' that is. This leads to something known in the trade as 'black and white thinking'. Basically any strong emotion focuses the mind, makes you more open to suggestion, and it makes you stupid. When we count we engage the conscious mind. This is why hypnotists sometimes get people to count backwards; it's suggestive of a conscious mind shutting down. 99 - 98 - 97 -

Let me ask you some questions so that we can get an objective view of things. Write the answers down or make a memorised mental note. I want you to know specific things. You need to know exactly when you get angry. You are presumably not angry all the time.

1. In a usual day, as things stand up to this point, what % of the day are you angry? 20%? 10% 70%.
2. In a usual day for what % do you remain calm or thereabouts? Just guess these figures. Trust your instincts.
3. Okay, now how many times a day do you lose your temper?
4. Are their common triggers to temper flare ups or do you feel generally angry and prickly?
5. In a given week what things usually anger you? Be 100% specific. Write these down.
6. Can you stay away from any of these anger-inducing stimulus? At least till we get this problem sorted out?
7. Now, how angry do you get? This is the true rageometre: let me show you what I mean…

The Rageometre.

0: Chilled out/calm.

2ish: Irritated/pissed off.

5: Anger zone. Definitely angry. But immediate oral sex would be able to change your mood.

7. Boiling over (starting to lose it).

10. Blind fury - you have lost the plot! An anger attack is under way and must play itself out. Only horse tranquillizer can soothe you.

You may notice I'm not taking things seriously. I never took my clients' problems seriously. My job was to get rid of them. I never bought into an end-of-the-world mindset. All psychological blips can be overcome. You are human. Now, you haven't always been Mr or Miss Angry Bastard. So when did this problem start? When did you become a rageaholic?

BUT WAIT! WHO IS RH?

Someone who wants to help. I suppose in a way all the 'hypnotherapy' (you've got to call it something) sessions I carried out involved some sort of positive emotional adjustment. Confidence sessions, phobia removal, even addictions require a 'rebalancing' of emotional processes that leads to some sort of long-term 'equilibrium'; despite the inevitable ups and downs that any human life is faced with.

A lack of love from a parent will do you no favours, but childhood unpleasantries are not set in stone. The word 'stress' was entirely invented quite recently. It used to be called good old fear. Stress is a valueless word favoured by psychologists who are being 'objective'; whatever that word means.

The fact is that we, I, you, everyone practices some sort of emotional control/dampening every day of our lives. If you looked at most of my former clients they looked no more worried than anyone else. This is because by and large they weren't any more worried etc. They, unlike everyone else, had decided that enough was enough and they wanted to *feel better*.

Let me ask you a question: how specifically to you want to feel, most of the time? Confident? Calmer? Happier? A combination of the 3? Let's take the first 3 letters C, C, H. That's what we'll aim for: CCH. Might as well call it that as anything. But you'll also need a flexibility of approach to problem solving, no more raging your way through life's upsets. You'll need to use your creativity more often: that will require you to keep your shit together. Ever tried painting a picture when seething with anger? Not gonna happen. You might manage some angry splodges I guess.

The Rogue Hypnotist was a successful NLP Master Practictioner and clinical hypnotherapist. He doesn't see clients anymore. He's writing books to help people through the curent crisis and learning CGI so he can set up his own animation company.

When he, I, was helping suffering clients, I achieved a 100% success rate with all my motivated clients by the time I left the field of 'therapy'.

To be fair there isn't much I don't know about hypnosis. But you don't need a deep hypnosis session with me in order to get what you want, natural hypnosis happens whenever you want to change things. You focus in to learn some new stuff that will give you new skills. People that have had 'anger problems', whatever, up till now,tend to bang their head up against the proverbial brick wall. After reading this book you will have a far greater array of tricks to get what you want more easily.

I have written about suggestion, persuasion, cults, and cultural hypnosis: you need not have read any of my other books to get what you desire from this one. Are you ready? Too late we already started a chapter ago. I'm a tricksy fellow...

'MR MCGEE, DON'T MAKE ME ANGRY. YOU WOULDN'T LIKE ME WHEN I'M ANGRY.'

Anyone who loved the original Bill Bixby, Lou Ferrrigno Incredible Hulk TV show knows that line. Bixby's delivery was perfect. But seriously: who likes you when you're angry? Not a pretty look is it? If I was to film you in a full on rage attack, what would you look like? How is everyone else reacting? Do you want to be known as Mr/Miss/Mrs Angry?! Please say no.

The fact is human anger is a posturing device before violence. Not always, but mostly. Most animals that feel threatened posture. They make themselves bigger. Snort. Stamp. Bark. Roar. Make loud noises. They may charge. The point of an anger display is to scare someone, something into submission, or make them back off. This can have its uses. But not everyday. Over trivial issues. Is your life on the line when you get angry? Do you need to physically fight? Do you need that adrenaline to hit someone? The answer is probably not. Funnily enough most people get angry over literal hot air: words.

Words are enormously powerful things. They are potentially more dangerous than nukes. They've certainly killed more people.

They can hide truth. They cause no end of trouble. Some people take them literally. Ah, words, we'd be lost without 'em, but...

Words are the tools of change in a very real way; they are in fact a technology, though often not thought of in that manner. All emotional states can and are altered by words; which are just symbols. The deepest layers of your mind processes information as metaphorical narrative symbols. Stories we tell ourselves. You may believe in a story, a linguistic curse, that you are an 'angry person'. No one is an angry person. Anger is something you feel at specific times and places, with specific persons. It is an evaluation of a situation that somehow you or something you value are under threat and you must unleash a counter-attack to protect it/you/them etc. That's a good intention. Keep the intention. We just need to make the responses more nuanced in future.

For example, do you know that is is possible to stop emotions by simply refusing to feel them to the same degree? At some level you need to realise that **you can consciously control emotions.** This requires a simple change of attitudes, new, slightly more sophisticated perspectives. These will put *you in control of what you feel* more often. Basically you need to *become calmer, and more creative.* You need *more flexibility of response.* This is all 100% learn-able. In fact you've done it already, haven't you? You have been flexible. You have been calm. You have been creative. All these things are already within you. You just need to access them more often. That is doable. All you need to *solve this problem* is within you. That should make you *feel happier* already.

Now, we need to talk about hypnosis, what it really is. Why it helps us change. It's time for each and both of you to realise that at some level you have to *refuse to get as angry* as you did back then. Enough is enough. You need to *take in things* that are actually important in any situation. You need to *let past, unhelpful fixations go*. With you, all is well. Trust that.

HYPNOSIS AND EMOTIONAL CONTROL.

Funnily enough the very part of our brain that is linked to our emotions is also linked to the state of hypnosis. Hypnosis can be used to elicit ANY emotional state whatsoever. What we call the 'subconscious' mind, for convenience, is the seat of our emotions. Our emotions help us evaluate ongoing experience. If someone is mean to us we feel anger and hate. Kindness is met by a feeling of love, fondness, warmth. Calmness is an emotion just as much as all the other many feelings we have. We tend to *feel calm* when there is no threat or stress. Then we feel comfortable. And we also feel like that after we have carried out something exhilaratingly physical like sex or exercise. The latter being the best natural stress reducer, eliminator, and soother that is known to man. It's a great way to stay fit, strong, and energetic. Have you noticed you're more likely to get angry if you are tired?

When we become angry we do indeed enter a kind of intense waking trance: our attention is focused solely on the source of anger. We do not pay much attention to anything around us in that state, including reason. It is a powerful state because it potentially keeps us alive, it helps us survive. But if you can't control it, it can get you into a lot of trouble. Most non-psychopaths who become violent are angry before a physical fight breaks out.

Fights are interesting things; they are not like the ones in the movies. Which are more like dances. Real 'fights' are often over in a matter of seconds. One person physically asserts dominance over another. But fights are risky - you can accidentally hurt someone badly. And you too may get badly hurt. Once fights escalate they have a way of getting chaotically out of control. If the fight is extremely violent you may become traumatised. How about a long vacation/holiday in prison? Sound like fun?

When angry we look at people like we want to fight them: we intimidate them. This to get them to back down. This can be 'fine' when appropriate. But daily life is no fun on a war footing. Moreover, those around you will soon get sick and tired of your stress tantrums. I bet you clench your fists. Your shoulders hunch. You shout. Are abusive. Bark orders. Your fuse is short. And after these attacks you feel like shit. You feel guilty. This isn't the real you. This is the effect of stress and worry on the human brain and nervous system.

Fortunately just as your nervous system knows how to pump you up for actions it also instinctively knows how to calm you right...down...All the way down. That's it. Think about it: what calms you down? Something has to change doesn't it? Perhaps you *see things in a new way*. Maybe someone makes you laugh in spite of yourself. Whatever it is. That old pattern is interrupted and the old signals don't fire off so intensely do they?

Have you ever gone for a walk somewhere that made you *feel very calm indeed*? Have you ever been so focused on something that you began to *feel contentedly calm*? Of course you have, we all have. And isn't that a wonderful feeling? You know there is what you might call a 'mind rule', I say it in most of my books, I didn't originate it, but it is true: **you get more of what you focus on.** I think, and each and both of you know, that it's time to focus more on what you really need as a unique individual living this life. Life is an ongoing challenge. We are tested in many ways. And we all deal with that best - 99.9% of the time - when we are *calm* in such a way that our creativity can kick in. You see it is *your calm emotional state*, which is again controlled by your subconscious, *your unconscious,* other-than-conscious processes, that allows that creativity to operate. For that to happen you need to *be much calmer overall* than you had been, wasn't it? And couldn't you? That's right.

A word about what we call 'hypnosis' for some reason or other. The word means *sleep.* But it isn't *sleep,* which is a form of *deep rest.* Hypnosis is a state of intense focus in which you can communicate with your deeper mind, your far deeper mind, now. In that place you can more readily daydream without any distractions. All you need do is zero in on something that interests you. That fascinates you very deeply. What positive things are you interested in? What things super fascinate you?

Have you ever had the experience of being deeply absorbed in anything? This is what it's like for me when I watch a good movie...

The outside world ceases to exist for a while. I am only aware of those big images. The sounds. The characters. The action. The special effects. That becomes your world for a while. You absorb the ideas and themes that are dramatised by the story...

When we read anything that absorbs us we *enter a trance state.* A waking trance state. Now, it can be of varying depths. Whatever is appropriate to help you *learn,* really learn, in a very real way that causes delightful change. Good information produces positive change. That's all that most hypnosis sessions are. The learning of helpful information. Practising doing things in ways that make you feel good, more often. That's the way.

Any activity that causes a pleasant state of concentration is hypnosis. Hypnosis is *focus.* Sometimes in focused states we pleasantly daydream. About anything helpful. New ways of doing things or ways we have done things and can associate to more often, again, when needed. All you need is already within you. And at a far deeper level you know this, do you not?

All children daydream. It's natural. As a child we daydream about anything. It's a way of taking a *rest,* a pause, relaxing and reflecting. Imagining and learning. Creating new things. Combining certain things in new ways. New connections form. You daydream when *you are calm and safe.* You can *relax* more, knowing a part of you is always looking out for danger, it does that unconsciously. So you can get on with life. You can deal with all of life's challenges. You are a doer. A problem solver. We all are. A part of you will solve problems easily, outside of awareness: so *you can relax* about that too.

The funny thing I learnt as a pro hypnotist is that an unconscious mind can *go into a healing hypnotic trance* state whenever it wants, when it thinks it is appropriate to do so. And that's a nice thing to know. Some people say that they read this series of books and *go to sleep*, waking up, somehow changed. There is a deeper magic...And it's not out here...it's always been inside of you...

CAUSES OF FRUSTRATION.

If you can't get what you want in a reasonable time you will become frustrated and possibly, angry. Thwarted goals are one of the main causes of anger. This is especially so when you believe you deserve the goal. When you passionately want it. Yet...it 'eludes' your grasp. Elude literally means to be made a fool of. Often we delude ourselves as to what is possible. Not because you are incapable of getting it. No. Because there is something 'out there' that thwarts you. In many ways you are being played with.

Money: this is probably the biggest source of frustration in human history for most people who have ever lived. In a 'civilised' system having enough of it is a daily concern. A lack of sufficient funds to live a decent life is a major cause of anger for many people. This lack of money is designed into the system to keep the masses fearful and submissive. In a word controllable.

Unfairness: general unfairness in all human societies is so widespread that it would be ludicrous to pretend that it does not exist. It takes many forms, usually having to do with rewarding people who do not deserve it, and penalising people who do not deserve it. Unfairness causes justifiable anger.

Learning: it can be very frustrating to learn something new. There are a whole class of new ideas, jargon, and procedures to learn.

The path to mastery is seldom an easy one. Trying to become 'professional standard' at anything takes time, practice, and an ability to learn from mistakes. This learning curve itself can make one angry. Much information must be paid for. The quality of training varies greatly. A good teacher/mentor is often pot luck. Access to the best information and teachers is usually bought at a high price. That many can't afford. This lack of access can cause mass resentment.

Dating/sex: the search for sex, love, a life partner can often seem harder than the search for Spock! There is a great competition to attract mates that is seen throughout the animal kingdom. Man is no exception. Add to this that most people in West World now do not marry. Promiscuity is the norm: this leads to an inability to pair bond. People now stay single for such a long time that our ancestors would have thought us mad. Many people lack any natural desire to commit. Divorce is rampant. The search for 'the one' and the failure to locate them in a timely way can cause a great deal of upset and anger.

Goals: everyone has goals, whether this is day to day problem solving or the desire to climb the ladder of success in varying fields. As in mate selection there is a great deal of competition. Much of the game of life is rigged by the rich and powerful for the benefit of their worthless offspring. Many people believe that you have to shit on others to get ahead. Some people will do anything to have their place in the sun. Goal achievement frustration is very common: even if you have the ability to achieve X, Y, Z there may be very many real prejudices that prevent you from doing so. The irrationality in the minds of men is the biggest obstacle to goal satisfaction. These irrational realities cause a great deal of anger. It is widely recognised that much 'success' is wholly undeserved.

Corruption: is the norm. Pathocratic societies, such as all the countries that currently compose what I dub 'West World', are dys-functioning at peak levels of corruption. It is hard to quantify but West World may be the most corrupt socio-cultural-political system in human history that we know of. All the bureaucracies and institutions are corrupt. Governments lie and manipulate as a matter or course: they are quite obviously at war with the mass of the populous. They wage wars for fictitious reasons endlessly. They introduce measures that impoverish the vast majority of people. The average person's standard of living is plummeting whilst a tiny minority lives high on the hog. For some reason this state of affairs makes some people somewhat testy.

Ideological/culto-religious: we live in an age of mad ideas. Ideas in fact so mad that to have possessed them in former times would have led people with nets to chase you down the street. Being mad is now the new 'sanity'. When civilisations fall they are often overtaken by a deluge of irrationalisms that infect the human psyche on mass. All ideologies, cults etc. force a schizophrenic template on reality and expect it to conform to sheer madness. When this occurs it is a sign that you are living at the end of an age. The madness of the cultic mindset angers a great many people who are sane. The trick is to retain your sanity at such times when the majority are running around like headless chickens. This is 100% doable.

Ageing: there can be much anger in growing old. The body doesn't quite do what it did easily, once upon a time. Older people are no longer respected or thought wise - a Children of the Corn sub-cult worships the genius of the inexperienced, easily-misled fool. Medical treatment for older folks is starting to resemble something between Soylent Green and Nazi Germany. The old are seen as a pair of old shoes - once useful, now disposable. 'Do not resuscitate' orders. The young do not seem to have any awareness that sooner than the imagine they too will be old. The world is going down the toilet and the old know it. What did they struggle for?

Youth: there is much anger in youth. The youth sees all the things that are wrong and wonders why they have not been put right. This natural urge to improve that the young possess is easily tricked into aiding and abetting those who created the problem in the first place. Having no experience of those who lie and make false promises they are easily led by the nose. Having known nothing but school life they believe the fantasies that monkish school teachers pump into their eager heads. This leaves them with a great disadvantage in the real world which more closely resembles a perverse pit of tigers than a school yard. Young men can be jeed up to fight wars for a whole host of made-up reasons. The young do not think of death. Or the realities of living the rest of your life physically and psychologically impaired. Society is filled with many Pied Pipers. The clash of programming with reality, and the realisation you were conned can be a great cause of vexation. And so it should be...

The reader may see the above list, which is hardly as long as it could be, as a justification for anger. Mass anger in fact. Anger is often justified, the question is: will it ultimately get you what you want? Accept the intention - change the behaviour. When you do this you will get better results and be less angry. What this book will do is help you *see the world more calmly and realistically*. Then you will experience far less frustration. The wise do not anger easily...

DEVELOPING 'PSYCHOLOGICAL TOUGHNESS'.

What do I mean by being psychologically tough? Very simple. **_You must think for yourself._** No matter what anyone else believes they 'think'. Whatever anyone else does.

When we leave school we no longer have teachers to bully us into line: the media takes this role over. The job of the media is to mislead you. To make you believe in lies like truth. The medium of TV is highly hypnotic. Even fiction, especially fiction, is in fact used to programme you. To make you believe in nonsense. All 'art' is little more than some form of propaganda. It was ever thus.

People often become angry when they imagine that the maps installed in their heads, sometimes even with the best of intentions, are about as useful as having two four-foot long dicks on your head. With these faulty maps everything you do fucks up. This makes you angry. "I thought that if I worked hard..." Oh, that old chestnut. "I thought that if I was law abiding"...You did? How'd that work out? "I thought that If I..." No, my friend, the last bloody thing you've been doing is thinking. If that were not so you would not be here. All you have to do to access your 'psychological toughness' is *think for yourself*. And I know that you have thought for yourself. Gone against the grain when it was the right thing to do. Made good decisions - chains of them that optimise happiness in your life. Notice the good things. More and more, now...

It's time for a change. In order to be less frustrated you need to stop being so fucking naive. With that in mind...

ACTUALLY PAY ATTENTION TO REALITY.

Do you believe words and pictures or do you observe reality itself? From the dawn of time many 'great' minds have thunked 'great' thoughts; almost all of these turned out to be great waste of time. Actually they were total bullshit! What was the 'science' of yesteryear is the fairy tale of today.

You see 'our', I say our with a sense of irony, beliefs are like a mind-net that your brain places over reality. This net has a series of nodes that selectively edit out anything that does not match the patterns of that net. In other words delusional ideas stop you seeing reality for what it is. That is not very helpful.

You may have ideas in there such as

I could never do that.
The situation is hopeless.
I am a failure.

Could never do what exactly? What is stopping you? What is the situation precisely? In what sense do you mean it is 'hopeless'? What is specifically preventing you from taking actions to resolve the problem successfully?

However, angry people tend to have more shouty beliefs:

Why do people do things to annoy me!?!
Why won't this fucking X work?!
Why is EVERYONE so stupid!?
Why can't THEY see that X, Y, Z won't work?!
Why did that c*nt just drive her car so close to mine!

The anger state makes us a little bit paranoid. After all we see that we are under threat. Angry people often expect things to be perfect. PEOPLE WILL NEVER BE PERFECT. "Why can't you be more like this ideal person I have in my head?" Which is a bit control-freaky if you think about it. Have you noticed that in all the above angry statements someone else is to blame? At no point are you responsible. That makes you a victim. An angry person is someone who neuro-linguistically dis-empowers themselves. They literally curse themselves to feel bad.

Look, lots of people do annoying things. That's not the problem. The problem is your sense of humour has vanished. You are using an angry tone in your head. You are saying stuff that triggers the anger part of your brain to attack.

Try this: in your head now say: "Why do people do things to annoy me?!" in a really calm tone. Now say it in a happy tone. Now say it as though it strikes you as the funniest thing ever. There is no conspiracy to annoy you. Trust me most people are thinking about one thing: themselves. Often they don't know you exist.

If we swear in our heads we can often trigger anger or hate. Swear words are great. I use 'em often. You might want to clean up your head language when you are feeling any pressure. That will stop you accessing intense emotions.

You can also think about the reality of those anger-inducing thoughts. Is EVERYONE stupid? We all do stupid things from time to time. Everyone is a lot of people. It's probably just one person that's pissing you off. Anger is an inefficient emotion. It is a state that cause us to generalise wildly. Many people are caught up in their own stressed-out lives. They don't mean to do 'stupid' things. Many people are also brainwashed. Their brains don't work properly. When you realise that most people who have ever lived have been brainwashed you might have a bit more sympathy for your fellow man.

There are lots of bad drivers. There are a number of pricks. Pricks have cars. Sometimes people get careless. They daydream. They are not paying attention. This is reality. They have had a bad day. Knowing that there are a lot of people with problems out there should make you be on the lookout for bad drivers. Chances are you will encounter one every time you drive. If you are aware of this reality you can empower yourself by being more aware on the roads. In any situation see if you can take back some power instead of giving it away.

If you have an angry thought pop into your head, and if it's an unhelpful one I want you to examine it to see if it is really an accurate description of reality. Dissect it. Is there evidence to back that angry statement up?

People often use the word 'they'. Who are the 'they'? When you get specific the 'they' turn out to be a much smaller bunch of individuals than you might have imagined. Are there any verbal patterns that you use that make you angry? Another benefit of all this is that if you are calmly thinking about things you can't get so angry.

ANGRY PICTURES IN YOUR HEAD!

I am going to make a wild guess that sometimes you make yourself angry by seeing anger-inducing pictures in your head. Maybe your boss told you off yesterday. You see his stupid fat, red-faced head. You re-hear him shouting at you. This makes you feel angry + humilated again.

The answer is - don't do that: that thing has happened. What if you saw that person as a giant walking banana with lipstick on, carrying a wobbly bright green dildo. As that banana tells you off it speaks in the most ridiculous high-pitched voice you ever heard: this alternative imaginary event evokes another set of emotions entirely.

Annoying images can be made black and white. Shrunk small and shoved off into the distance. Notice if it is the something you show to yourself in your head that is making you angry, stressed, whatever: if it is use your creativity to *change that response*.

It's your private movie theatre: you choose the movies.

THE PHYSICALITY
OF ANGER.

Do people in a calm state shout? Does their face go red? Do they bare their teeth? Furrow their brow? Do they hunch their shoulders? Do they look at people in such a way as though it looks like they want a fight? Do they bark out words in a kind of staccato, machine gun fashion? Does their head jut forward? Do their fists clench? Do they growl? Do they stamp the floor? Do they throw things? Hit things? Do they roar? Do they generally have the appearance of a cornered dog? Are they rude? These are rhetorical questions: the collective answer is no.

A calm face is relaxed. Hands loose and free from tension. Standing up straight. Probably with a slight smile on the face. The body is relaxed. The voice is smooth and calm, confident, with enough breath support for the words. The person is both spontaneous and thinking. Aware of their surroundings. They look in control. Relatively serious and mature. They handle differences diplomatically and good-naturedly. They keep their temper.

Reimagining that response...

Can you imagine an apple? Get a real sense of it? Can you visualise a table with a bowl of apples on it?

Read this relatively slowly...Have you ever tried acting like *you're a calm person*? Let a pleasant image of a calm you come to mind. See yourself behaving in a calm grown-up fashion over there. If you know a calm person note how they behave. Learn from them unconsciously and quickly now. The mind can learn very quickly, much quicker than perhaps you know.

Now, after you have imagined a you behaving in a way you like, are impressed with, I want you to start that little mind movie again from your point of view. See through those calm and in control eyes. *Feel the confidence* and ease all throughout your body. Acting in a confident, I can handle anything kinda way. See the new, better responses you are getting from other people. See things as they are. No drama. Just living. Getting on. Enjoying yourself. Better company. The real you that was always there, deep down, underneath that past tension. Wasn't it? Didn't you? That's right. Take you time, at some level, to *imagine all this vividly*...

Good. Your far deeper mind can take this simple act as a sign and a signal that this is what you want more of in your much more enjoyable future.

See *a calm confident you* over there, just ahead in your mind's eye. They have all the resources they need to solve any solvable problem. They have changed in all the ways you need to, to get what you really want. When you're ready - step, float, whatever into that much calmer you...That's it. Notice how much better that feels. Let *all the appropriate learnings somehow take...*

Excellent! Now see an even more with it you. A person who is so *calm and in control, now* - simply not bothered by things that once fussed them. Notice how much better it feels from this position. *You are confident and happier.* Float into that you and simply absorb all you need to...

Okay. One last time for luck. When you're ready: see the most calm and confidently happy you. They have everything they need.

Unflappable. Good humoured. Good company. Wiser. Smarter. More fun. Water off a duck's back. So at ease. Challenges are there to be overcome. Much more energy...they have what you need...And now...float, walk, step into that new you. The real you. The person you deeply truly are. Deep inside. Locked in. Take...it...easy...tiger...And this is so. If you feel you wish to - read through this section again...And when you're ready...

Doing angry.

The acting teacher Stanislavski developed a techniques called the Method of Physical Actions. This stated that all emotion is expressed through behaviour. Take anger. Let's say you are in a play and have to pick up a frying pan and place it on a kitchen surface.

Now you could do that in a functional way, like you were trying to make scrambled eggs. But what if the playwright demands that the character you are playing is always impatient OR has just had a row/argument, whatever, with another character?

Well you might yank that frying pan out of that cupboard, pulling all the other pots and pans onto the kitchen floor. Now you've got that pan you smash it down hard onto the top of your oven. That is doing angry. You have a want - get pan. You do it a certain way using an adverb - angrily.

What if you are in a play. This play is called real life. To a certain extent it is a game. A bit like the movie Groundhog Day. Now, in this play that you are writing this character that you play never does things angrily. They do everything calmly. From now on you'll be doing calm. Or doing fun. Or doing happy. Or doing...well I'll leave that to each and both of you.

GOOD FOOD AND EXERCISE = CALMER.

For some reason modern man is not very modern. He or she thinks they don't have to stay fit, they don't have to exercise regularly. Say 3 - 4 days a week, breaking out in a light sweat. But as you are wiser now, you now know the 'I don't need to exercise' thing is a myth. Here's why.

Exercise removes stress chemicals from the body. There is a thing known terribly as 'allostatic load'. The wear and tear on the body and mind from stress. You can massively reduce allostatic load by regularly exercising in a way that's right for you. Walking is exercise. Sitting down all day isn't. Swimming is a great all body exercise.

Anxiety and depression (anxiety gone bonkers) 'sufferers' see a great improvement by simply exercising. This is because cortisol is broken down and removed by exercise. It's just one of the amazing things your body does if you meet its needs. You water plants and give them sunlight. I hope you do. Mushrooms can apparently live on shit, you can't, so...

Eat healthy too. All the food groups, including fat. You need carbs and protein, preferably from meat. Organic is best. Pesticides are not good for the body. They won't kill you immediately, but like smoking they won't do you any favours. The body and mind work best when free of nasty chemicals.

Zebras have a way of shaking out their allostatic load, we don't. We have to exercise. I had plenty of 'wine moms/mums' (it can be stressful to be a parent and to work too) come to see me. NONE EXERCISED. I suggested, in hypnosis, and it's only a suggestion, that they eat well. That they find an exercise routine that suits them as an individual. Because we are all very different. We all need to exercise but we don't all need to exercise in the same way.

You will enjoy how clear-headed and fresh you feel after exercise. You will feel better in general. You will feel far less stressed. And so the little diminishing anger monkey won't be able to get a foot in the door. You'll look sexier, be more attractive, brighter-eyed and more confident. I predict you'll *feel far happier*. Your walk will be bouncier and more optimistic. And the good thing is that change starts from the inside out. Give yourself the firm foundation of health that arises from a healthy diet and regular exercise. If you don't like the gym don't go. Cycling? A sport you used to like playing. To have the experience of change you must *commit at a very deep level* to experiencing certain new, better experiences, experientially. Now. Ah yes! The power of creativity.

GET CALM - GET CREATIVE.

Wouldn't it be a better response to *get creative* rather than angry in the face of a problem? Frustration = a problem. **All solvable problems can be solved given enough time.** A problem is an unwanted state now. But we can take action to overcome it.

Instead of flying off the handle and therefore shutting off your creative brain what if, when face with a frustrating situation, you generated 6 ways to get around it?

Our creativity has many functions. Yes, you can draw nice pictures or create new songs with it, and you can use it to solve problems for you. If you *get that* energy draining, creativity blocking *anger reaction out of the way.*

There have been times, have there not, when you used your creativity to solve problems? Contrary to myth everyone is creative. In fact, at an unconscious level, your deepest mind is working on solutions to challenges all the time. You can *relax*, go off and do something else, and when it's ready, those solutions will simply pop into consciousness. You just need to know that you have this ability - then trust it.

We can get in trouble when we invest a lot of energy on a very specific outcome. This is most obviously so in the case of unrequited 'love'; which is usually lust.

That person you are obsessing over may like you but they don't find you sexually attractive. It's just the way it is. I'm afraid you are going to have to get use to the idea that not everyone finds you attractive. If you calmed down - you'd realise they've done you a great big favour. Instead of moping, whining, and becoming a stalker you can now go and find someone who does find you sexy.

In 3 months time you won't even remember you were fixated on them because your life will have moved on. I have known men who were actually driven crazy by an ex who dumped them. In all cases these 'wonderful women' they were devoted to were psychos. This is another plank in fending off anger: don't make stupid decisions in the first place.

Keep your sense of humour in the face of disappointments. Keep things in perspective. Even in truly bad times your sense of humour will get you through. Humour is linked to creativity. We are much more creative when we are having fun. The idea of the 'tortured artist' is an idea promoted by psychopaths actually.

You must keep an emotional balance throughout the events of life. Life turds happen. Politicians both deliberately and due to incompetence fuck things up. Some people are rude, some stupid. Some brainwashed. Some are clueless, others prejudiced bigots. This is the reality of some humans. It is a part of life to learn to deal with this stuff.

The best way to deal with stuff is to get creative. You can strengthen your 'creative muscles' by doing more genuinely creative things. Draw, paint, write, sing in the shower, grow stuff in the garden, or on your apartment balcony. Reading novels is good for creativity.

Going for walks and even doing the washing up are physical activities that allow the mind to naturally wander and generate ideas.

The secret to creativity is to trust what the deep mind offers: don't censor it. This is a thing some 'shy' people do: an idea for a conversation is offered by the deep mind. Then the judgemental, scared part of them starts criticising it. Trust your subconscious, unconscious, whatever you want to call it: it knows more than you know consciously. It is bombarded with and contains vastly more data than consciousness can handle. The 'conscious' mind is a selective filtering mechanism.

I know some people who solve problems in their sleep, while they dream. The dreaming mind works on the solution and offers it to them in a dream. I know a childen's author who's brain does this for him.

One of the reasons people get 'frustrated' is that no one gives us a book as young children called 'how my brain works'. It knows how it works, but the conscious mind doesn't. This scares the conscious mind because it's a bit dumb at times. You don't need to know all the secrets of life or the mind. You just need to know that if you *remain calm* and focus - your mind is more than capable of being highly creative in a way that easily helps you solve many things in ways that please you.

BE PATIENT.

Impatience is caused by the idea that something must occur within a specific time frame. Indeed, sometimes this is the case. We must eat food and drink water after specific intervals or we get in serious trouble. But when you are at the gym and someone is using that piece of equipment you can be flexible, and perhaps wait a bit or work on another piece of equipment till so and so has finished. *Be patient* and you'll be far less angry.

You can't blame some people: there are social meta-programs that tell us we SHOULD do things at certain times. Says who? What are we clones who all do the same things, have the same goals, share the same principles? The fact is we are all vastly different. One of the major problems all humans face is 'group-think'. What we call group-think is actually brainwashing. The uncritical acceptance of ideas because lots of people or powerful people tell us something is so. Every great invention started off with only one person knowing something was so: the inventor.

There are 'yes' and 'no' cultures: America was, until recently, more of a yes culture than the Old World. People in yes cultures are more likely to experiment, try things out. Take risks. They are also more encouraging to people who want to attempt things out of the ordinary. When someone tries to limit the scope of your ambitions and imagination you do know what it occurring don't you? They are merely revealing to you THEIR OWN limitations.

There is another problem: we live in a now culture. Everyone wants everything now. The Internet has encouraged this trend.

Fast food didn't exist 200 years ago. Yet people got on. We expect postal deliveries yesterday! In part due to Amazon's ability to deliver stuff to us so quickly. This breeds impatience. Politicians demand obedience to their insane diktats now. Everything takes as long as it takes to get done. You can't instantly make a chair from Ikea or whatever - it takes time to assemble. Be patient.

Now sometimes we are kept in line too long and you are right to complain. But some people unrealistically get angry because they are frustrated that it takes time to learn a complex skill or skill set. They get angry if they make a mistake in a learning process: folks; *life is a learning process*. We never stop learning. Those who do stagnate. There is always more to know and experience. Getting heated about learning a skill that takes years to learn is a dumb waste of time and energy. Relax. You will get there. Your old anger was in fact slowing you down; which is ironic. Be patient.

And be patient with other people too. That teenager in McyDees or wherever doesn't deserve a shout rage because her manager is useless, or because retail corporation X, Y, Z has a stupid refund policy.

In London men in suits always moan at train guards because their train is late. Rather than complaining to the CEO who created a culture of terrible train services as the norm. Such stupid behaviour solves nothing and just pisses people off who aren't responsible. Be patient, be sane, be polite, be sensible. Remain calm. Shit situations are exacerbated by two things: panic and misdirected anger. Now it annoys me when people say 'keep calm and carry on' whilst civilisation circles the plughole of history but...Keep your shit together, especially during shit times. Tough times are the times that test us: you must pass the test. Don't implode or explode. It won't help; if it would help I'd say go for it. It doesn't. Be patient.

There are times to be impatient too; times when someone needs a kick up the butt, metaphorically speaking. When that's appropriate. Most of the time CHILL. We are more resourceful when we are calmer.

If you were a soldier and your general kept throwing rage fits every time a bomb hit would you have confidence in your 'leader'?

'MR/MRS/MISS REASONABLE'.

Some people are for some reason super-reasonable all the time. Well, most then. No matter what goes on they are always level-headed. If there is a situation that could escalate out of hand they'll always calm it down.

They provide good reasons for things rather than emotive slogans. They will often try to meet you half way and compromise if possible. They are stoical. Practical. They never back down. They are often beyond brave. They do the right thing fearlessly. Often lots of people admire this type. They are humane and make good, loving, supportive parents. They make good leaders.

They talk the talk and walk the walk. They almost never lose their temper. If they do something must have really pissed them off. It must be important enough for them to show displeasure. People take such people seriously. Have you noticed Mr and Mrs Angrys are kinda a bit weird and hysterical? They seem intimidating at first. But it's just hot air. They look unbalanced. Their eyes bulging, speaking without enough breath. Hardly a person to inspire confidence.

Trying to control others by making them scared has several results: everyone thinks you're a prick and says so behind your back. They will eventually rebel. You will lose allies. No one will think you are a serious, grown-up person. Do you know red (if you're white), angry, shouty faces are hard to look at? They look ugly. They move too quickly. Look stressed - hardly true leadership traits.

Mr and Mrs Reasonable's skin tone stays even, they look composed, confident, on top of things. They never act aggressively or in an intimidating way: why? It makes you look weak. Power comes from stillness not rage. Hotheads scare the timid. Someone will always call your bluff sooner of later.

Reasonable types listen. Hotheads demand you listen to them only. Which type seems more appealing? Even if you add a dash of Reasonable to your behavioural portfolio I bet, overall, you get better results in general.

You are not your emotions. No more than the sea is always stormy or always calm. Boats bob up and down in all conditions. We never think of the sea's natural state as being waves crashing. Lighting striking. Brooding, rainy clouds. All this brouhaha passes in time. The sea is calm once more. Is that not so?

EXPECTATIONS
AND ANGER.

We often expect too much from others. As though we hold them to far higher standards of ideals than we hold ourselves. "He doesn't work hard enough!" This could be true BUT is it? "You must always turn up on time!" What if the train drivers are on strike? What if there was a multi-car pileup on the motorway/freeway?

"You didn't have that report on my desk on time!" Reply: "I was ill." People get ill. Some people get angry because they have staff that put their children's needs before their employers. Yes? And? That's the way it's supposed to be. You're supposed to put kids first. Underlying this is the childish notion that: the world isn't doing exactly what I want!!! Correct. And?

"He doesn't agree with me!" He has that right. "She never listens to what I say!" Then why bother talking to her?

Are your expectations of other too demanding? People can only do, can only give what they are capable of giving. Most people do their best. They are not being mean, spiteful, lazy, whatever. It may come as a surprise but others DO put their needs first. Don't they? Shit happens. It is what it is. And since that is so: what possible use is all that useless anger? It's pissing you off. Let...it...go. No one is perfect. You aren't or you wouldn't be here. Why must everyone else be?

If you are starting to get angry STOP and ask: are my expectations of this person and this situation too high? If the answer is yes: calm...yourself...all...the...way...down. See the world and what is in in with a clear head. You can talk away that annoyance. THINK.

KEEP YOUR PASSION.

People who regularly feel angry are often passionate people. They feel very strongly about things; often they are opinionated and outspoken. There is nothing wrong with any of that.

There is a time for passion. Imagine how dull life would be if we felt nothing. If you were just a lifeless husk with no emotional responses. That would be horrible. Be thankful and appreciative that we have such a wide emotional range. Emotions are wonderful things that at times we feel deeply.

Anger can well up and peak, cool down, and then flare up. I bet you are capable of a deep intensity of feeling: when you love you love wholeheartedly and deeply. When you hate you really hate. When you have fun and laugh you do so to the max. It is a good thing to be a passionate person.

The problem is specific: too much anger, probably too intensely, for too long a period of time. Getting aches and pains in the neck and shoulder area. The only thing you need to do is chill on the anger. Keep anger, but less often, less intense, for shorter periods.

Do you get angry when the following things are missing:

Good company.
Healthy food.
Privacy.
A meaningful work life.
Good night's sleep.
Fresh air.

Exercise.
Your safety feels threatened.
People don't appreciate you.
You don't feel accepted.
Not getting enough positive attention.
Unable to give others positive attention.
You feel you lack respect or recognition.
You feel you are not achieving things you actually value.
Your life is not sufficiently purposeful.
You feel you lack meaningful experiences.

That anger will inevitably dissipate when: you spend more time with people who 100% appreciate you. When you *live a life of true purpose* in which you have a far greater degree of control. When you take your physical needs seriously. When you have at least some time to commune with yourself. To reflect and ponder. In other words what you need to do is...

LIVE A MORE FULFILLING LIFE.

Imagine how your innate passion would then be directed into positive channels. Frustration would lessen considerably and you'd find *far less anger* events occurring. The only person that can make this happen is YOU.

ANGER AND 'DEPRESSION'.

It is often stated that people with so-called 'depression' often have 'anger issues'. If you couldn't get to sleep, worried practically all the time, and more than likely had some un-dealt with background trauma you might be a tad angry. I can only refer readers with depression to my book **Hypnotically Annihilating Anxiety**. This provides a comprehensive picture of what depression really is and how to 'treat' it. By that I mean get rid of it for good. However, all of the tips in here will help you too, so keep reading...

ANGER AND TIME.

Time pressures are more likely to make us angry. Thinking that an unpleasant situation will last for a long time will make us angrier. You can tough out a few minutes, but a week, a year? Time speeds up for many when they're angry. That's because it's an urgent survival emotion.

Give...yourself...enough time. Trust that you can and will solve any solvable problem - no matter how long it takes. Your focus is solving the problem. It takes as long as it takes. That's reality. SLOW...RIGHT...DOWN. Angry thoughts are fast. Chill. If you think an angry thought slowly it'll make you less angry...I'm.........really.............angry. Oooh! You sound it.

What if you gave yourself more time. Take more time to do fun things. Don't spend most of your precious time overworking. Focus more on doing more things, more often that make you *feel good*. If you give that old anger habit less time it will...fade...away...

Lacking time?

Time is funny, it exists out there as a measurement based on the sun's movements etc. The earth's rotation etc. The changing seasons etc. But mostly time exits in HERE. Time is how we perceive what we call TIME. The riddling element.

Do you recall the long day of childhood? You just have all the time in the world. The day lasts forever. At some point time started to speed up. Sooner or later you felt like a buzzing fly or bee. And worse still as time sped up you lost time. You didn't seem to get so much done. You have less time with the family. The kids are growing up and you hardly see them. STOP THAT WATCH!

I had hypnosis clients with 'time problems': I'll say to you what I said to them, in trance...

"Your unconscious mind 100% controls your sense of time passing. It knows all the psychological-perceptual components of all the ways you experience time. You will find in the time that is upcoming that you have, for some unfathomable reason, much more time. You are getting more done. You therefore feel a greater satisfaction. You use time well. As it's agreeable, a part of you that does so can make certain changes at a very deep level that alters time in a way that gives you more time..."

And this is so.

THE STORY OF THE OLD WARRIOR.

In those days there was once an old warrior of great renown. He had fought many battles, won many wars. He had medals and trophies. Many lords and kings had given him castles, land, animals, gold, even people in thanks.

His war-like spirit had served him well. Had got him through some very tough times. On the battlefield he had been a raging lion, people feared him. His banner alone struck fear into his enemies. It was said of him that he was a hot-head; always looking for trouble and a fight. It was all he had known.

But one day he realised that his bruised and battered war- scarred body was too old to keep continuously fighting. He was feeling tired. His body ached. He wanted a rest. So he hung up his sword. Locked it in his armoury and swore never to take it out again.

For years he lived happily. In his new state he began to notice many things that had formerly evaded him. Everyone noticed how much kinder the old warrior was. He had grown richer through his new wisdom. People from many lands came to him for advise. For he had learned the greatest mystery of all: the secrets of living well.

A year and one day passed. An invading force was reported on the borders of the kingdom. The old warrior got his key. He was polishing his old sword when his wife run toward him in great distress. "Please my husband, put back your sword. Leave the battle to younger knights!"

The old warrior laughed and kissed her cheek. "Fear not my dear. I have learnt the ways of peace, but my old sword I will keep for trouble."

DON'T GET RID
OF ANGER.

Some 'NLP' courses offer their students a way to 'get rid of anger'. Why would you want to do that? If you trip over, do you cut your leg off? Of course not because that would be stupid.

Anger serves a very powerful purpose. We all need anger in some situations. You know when and what these times are. There is a time for the appropriate level of anger.

If someone does something that crosses one of your red lines you have a right to get angry. Getting angry about things that piss you off is a human right. It's wired into you. Thank goodness. Perhaps you could turn the volume or scale of it down at times?

All animals have displays that warn other living things that there are some things that they will not put up with. These displays give others pause for thought. If behaviour X continues to be emitted there will be consequences that you might not like. For example everyone has the right to protect themselves from predators.

You have boundaries: people have no right to cross them. No one has a right to rig a game. No one has a right to accuse you unjustly. What you think and feel matters. If others don't appreciate these realities, well, they are going to have to learn. Perhaps the hard way.

Anger is like fear, it's your friend, but like fear don't let it become your boss.

JUST REFUSE!

Do not underestimate the power of refusal. What if you simply refused to get angry? What if that led you to succeed 99% of the time. What if you worked out your own tricks and methods of diffusing tension? What if you de-escalated, rather than escalated? What if you felt that old anger niggle rise up and you said - NOPE! I have found some better ways. I don't need to do that as often as I did. I am more sophisticated now. I refuse to go back to the old ways. I have grown tired of doing that. By trying to make others feel bad to get what I want I ended up alienating them and making myself feel bad more than anyone else. For entirely selfish reasons I denounce that old anger habit. In fact I refuse to call it anger - it is rhubarb. I refuse to eat any more rhubarb!!!

As a child you may have cried and cried and then one day you just got sick of crying all the time and said to yourself. I am not doing that anymore. Have there been times in your past when you resolved to put a stop to something? At a deep level you know what you did. We all have unconscious mechanisms of control, moderation, and change. The power to *become more emotionally mature and appropriate*. To find wiser ways to get what you want. And there is a part of you that will help in all of this in some mysterious ways that you need not even understand, consciously.

Remember: I refuse.

If you *simply refuse* you will find another way...

I'M BEING TREATED BADLY.

You are not anybody's punch bag. There have been many societies that scapegoated certain groups. Most, if not all, were run by a ruthless dominant minority that lorded itself over its 'slaves'. They often treat the majority to regular doses of state terror and legalised theft. Wealth has been 'redistributed' for ever. Usually to the thieves of the world.

There are many injustices that certain people see as 'justice'. Nobody should accept being treated badly. When did everyone stop judging individuals as just that? When did merit, talent, and ability become totally unimportant? Why do we fail to accurately assess the actual person in front of us? Don't we all deserve to be judged by who we really are, and not how people hallucinate we aren't?

Some people refuse to see the good in good people. That is a shame. And a foolish one at that. There are consequences to actions. I once knew a woman, who knew someone that had a 'mother'. I say a 'mother' because she didn't act in any kind of motherly way. She had 3 daughters. One she ignored. One she was pleased by because she always did well at school. The third was actively picked on and told she was stupid and worthless. It's a familiar story unfortunately.

This 'mother' did 'provide' the material things for her daughters. But she could not love. You see she/it was quite dead on the inside. But the girls never knew. They were after all little girls who rightly expected to be loved. Not one of the 3 was left unscathed. Children who are picked on often think that THEY are to blame for not being loved. But for a human it is impossible not to love your own children. It is a shame but flesh sacks without a soul or a conscience may also give birth.

Surviving this unpleasant situation is one thing. Learning from it is very important. Never let anyone treat you badly. Not for one second. If you do, they will get addicted to it, and come back for more. You deserve the respect everyone should get. You deserve to love and be loved. You deserve your talents to be recognised: one way or another. You deserve more than you've been getting. You deserve to *feel a sense of contentment* that you have worth, are a good person. You deserve the right to be judged accurately: for who you are, and only EVER that.

When you realise that you deserve the best you will *calm down*, let that old resentment go, and live a life that is increasing filled with more joy, more love than you ever believed, even through harder times. When are times not hard for a lot of people? *Reconnect to your inner strength.* We all 'get through'. But more than that, don't just get through: do it in style...

By the way no one turned up to the 'mother's' funeral.

ANGER ROBS YOU OF ENERGY.

We are living through created crisis after created crisis. Stay calm. There are many things to get justifiably angry about. The problem is that anger will be wasted. It will be the equivalent of shouting at the TV or banging your head against a brick wall. In other words - what's the point?

When you are stressed you waste energy that you will need to deal with the very real crisis that we will all live through for the next decade +. That's reality. My advise is: keep your energy to take measures that will help you survive and thrive. None of us can afford to indulge in over-emotional hysteria. Hysteria simply makes people make stupid decisions. You must make decisions coldly at times, simply based on facts that pertain to actual reality.

This is no time for indulging in fantasy thinking. Fantasy thinking leads to warped expectations and over-emotionalism. Do not pay attention to the unending 'fear-porn' promoted by the media. If you take it seriously you will lose your emotional equilibrium and make stupid decisions. As far as is humanly possible *remain calm*: these are the times that test men's souls. This is a testing time: you must pass the test if you want to survive. And we will survive the current crisis by using our heads. Remember that no matter what governments imagine - you are their boss, not the other way around. Keep your energy and keep your power.

SEXUAL FRUSTRATION AND ANGER.

No one really likes to talk about this but sexual frustration can be a big cause of anger. This is more overtly evident in men, who will even fight over females. The fact is adults need sex quite regularly. Sex makes the world go around. The best way to actually have a good sex life is to find a loving life companion.

It is far easier for women to get laid than men: they just have to show up. Men will be more attractive if they 1. Act like men. 2. Act responsibly and maturely - have your shit together. 3. Never act desperately: ever. 4. You will have more success with women if you are capable of ignoring them. Do not lavish a woman you don't know with unearned attention. She gets lots of attention, which flatters her ego, multiple times every day in her prime. 5. Act as if you have self-respect. 6. Know that women enjoy sex more than you. 7. Live your passion - men who are successful are attractive. 8. Never seek a woman's approval. At least not until you're in a proper relationship. 9. Have a job and some money. 10. Owning a car, although not 100% necessary never hurt any man's sexual chances. At some point a woman will expect you to drive her places. Are you going to piggyback her on days out? Get real my son.

If you follow these guidelines alone you will do better with the chicks. Ladies don't really need advice on this shit. My only advice for women is: ladies, stay away from losers. Have babies...

DON'T BLAME YOURSELF.

Lost opportunities. If onlys. I should have. Maybe if I had. Anger at what has happened can't be altered unless you invent a time machine, and, er...How much time do we waste getting angry about things that have happened? How much anger is vented on an often imaginary, fabricated past? What we call 'the past' often only exists as a 'recording' - in the head, as memories. Out there in various media. In books which are words that pose as facts. Words are tools for obtaining objectives: current and future objectives.

Getting angry over the past will not change what happened. If it happened. It will make you angry now. Anger with no outlet chews up the person who feels it now. The person/s who did this or that are off feeling whatever, not caring how you feel. They may even be dead. Before you die realise that life is for living. You do know that bitterness only makes you feel bad.

We develop habits of mind and body. If you had an old resentment tape/loop/pattern it may be time to let...it...go. You don't have to forgive or forget. But you do have to live with yourself and others now. Shouldn't you have more fun now? What will be better about your future when you focus on anticipating problems that can be solved, whilst you successfully solve problems? Learn all you need to learn from that stuff back then, then move on. These learnings become the unconscious matrix of better decisions that make a better you have a better future. You take more opportunities when they arise. 'If only' becomes 'I did it'. You will do many amazing things: do you think you've had all of your best experiences yet? Oh, my sweet summer child. Keep inventing...

ARGUE AWAY ANGER.

Do you ever argue with yourself in your head? Course you do, we all do. If you were what you believed was an 'angry person' you must be very good at arguing. Have you ever thought about arguing away your anger?

If you feel a surge of anger perhaps you could say,

"Oh not you again. Go away!"

"It's not that bad. Calm down and think about this logically."

"Is this really worth getting that angry about?"

"Stop being so aggressive. It isn't helping."

It is hard to get really angry if a critical part steps in and plays the role of referee, saying essentially: CALM DOWN. When you calm down and THINK you'll solve the problem. NLP calls this a pattern interrupt. Since all internal events are a process, a series of steps, if you add in or subtract a step then that old behavioural loop cannot function. Try it.

As in private therapy work I would sling out a lot of ideas to my clients. I told them, "If this works use it, if not don't. These are just ideas. Take the ones that feel right and ignore the other ones." I always found that overwhelming a problem with possible solutions is better than only having one.

Parts work.

Now I know that there is a part of you that is responding in a certain way. Thank you for what you did. I know there is another part that wants to do some new things. Wants to experiment and see if it can get better results. The good thing is both parts have the same intention: they are merely using differing strategies to get good results. At an unconscious level. The conscious mind need know nothing about this, because now I am speaking to your subconscious mind only...I would like all relevant parts to come to some sort of agreement to *do things in a new way*. A way that works better, makes this person far happier. Negotiations can be a very good thing. When all parts of you pull in the same direction you will find that you *get much better outcomes*. Challenges are easier to overcome.

A creative part of you will need to become involved, offering possible strategies, new ideas that can be tried out. Life is an ongoing experiment in living. And the core of who you truly, deeply are can oversee the whole process; after all it knows what is in your highest interests. Cohesion = success.

ANGER IN RELATIONSHIPS.

Some people get off on anger. I was walking along, once upon a time, and up ahead I heard the voice of a young woman arguing, turns out on the phone. Turns out with her boyfriend. And she loved it! She was getting off on it.

I think a lot of blame for this stupid type of new addiction must be directed at those late 20th century TV shows which get a bunch of low IQ, mentally ill fruitcakes, with a whole host of 'issues', throw them on a stage and watch them let rip at each other. That's entertainment. The problem is there is an unspoken, presupposed meta-suggestion about anything on TV: know what it is? It is the first commandment of TV. Anything and anyone that is on TV is copy worthy. You should emulate their behaviour.

Think about it, people had been conditioned to think that the old Hollywood stars were the height of fashion, great intellectuals (stifle laugh here), you name it. If you read lines and didn't bump into the furniture you could do no wrong. Be careful what you copy.

I had a young woman who came to see me because as a child she had seen her mum/mom run for her life at the sight of a teeny-tiny English spider. Now indigenous English spiders are so un-dangerous that...We don't have black widows or those giant Australian spiders that apparently lay in wait in toilets and bite your ass. We learn all kinds of odd behaviours through simple imitation. This goes on for most people throughout life. They never stop imitating others.

You even get it with mothers who copy their daughter's fashion tastes. It's not always bad. But what is bad is a pattern of habitual, repeated angry interactions in the home. At the workplace. On the street. People are much less polite and pleasant now than the used to be. Many people believe they have a right to get angry and even attack complete strangers for no good reason at all. They just feel entitled to do it. A large number are willing to kill a person who 'makes' them angry. Mass irresponsibility is a contemporary habit.

Good relationships should be based, primarily, on an assumption of mutual 'I mean you no harm'. This is the basis of basic true trust. Who trusts someone who loses their temper too often? Shouts and screams. Calls people they supposedly 'love' nasty names? Who wants to live in that kind of atmosphere? Life is hard enough without making it unnecessary harder. The home should be a haven.

Abusive anger has no real place in good relationships. Now we all get angry; but taking it out on those you love is dumb. Not only that, your spouse, boyfriend/girlfriend, partner, whatever, might just up sticks and leave you. They may have had just enough of you and your self-indulgent outbursts. Don't go out of your way to make other people's lives more shit than they might already be. There is an old NLP pattern, some people call it 'The Scrooge' pattern.

I had a man who was squandering family money on drugs. His kids were going without. The family finances were now tight. His wife warned him to straighten himself out or she might leave. As he told me this he was laughing. To himself. He wasn't taking it seriously. My 'diagnosis' was that I was dealing with an immature dick. He was not facing reality. In hypnosis I made him do so.

Facing the consequences of anger.

Imagine 6 months from now that you have not faced up to that anger problem....Things have gotten much worse in your life. What things will happen if you don't *sort this out*? Has someone you cared for gone their own way? Has your health suffered? Are you more frustrated? Think of where there are stresses now caused by that old anger pattern you had. How might they develop in ways that deeply displease you? Ponder that...

Now imagine 1 year from now. How much worse has your life become? When you fail to solve a problem all that happens is that you store up even more problems. The size of your problem ball gets bigger and bigger. Could your anger problem get you in legal trouble? Could you lose your job? Look at the faces of the people you have hurt with that former way of being. Isn't it time to say, finally, that *enough is enough*? When *you are determined to change* you will find that all the parts of you will assist you. Really visualise how bad your life will be one year from now if you miss this opportunity to *creatively change*.

Now one last time: it's two years from now. What kind of shit space have you gotten yourself into? If you didn't do it - who did? Everyone gets frustrated, feels ignored, unhappy, stressed, overworked, feels the pinch of undeserved financial pain BUT exploding is not the way to *solve those things intelligently*. I don't know you, so I don't know specifically how your life could go that wrong. You do. Vividly imagine what might happen if you made the mistake of failing to *change things now*. You owe that to yourself and others....

We have a saying in England, "Fuck that for a game of soldiers!" this loosely translates into - "I don't want that to happen!"

Okay. Now the good thing is that like Dicken's Scrooge none of that really occured. Resolve now that you can, will, and have *put all that behind you, now.* You are the master of your emotions. All emotions can be controlled. There are things you can do, consciously and unconsciously to *feel more in control* of so many differing things. The first step is to want this.

The second step is to commit to this. Then comes a new philosophy of living which only you can decide upon. New attitudes, beliefs, behaviours, more of one feeling or more, less of others - diminishing...away...If something isn't getting you the result you wish for - change what you're doing. Difference leads to difference. Same leads to same. At a deep level I want a part of you that does such things to know, really know, exactly what has to change. That talking bit doesn't even have to know. You know.

Your stubborn part will certainly assist. You are more creative that you knew. It is better to adapt than 'cope'. Every problem can be solved. Accept what you can't change. Change what you can. Keep making improvements. The small adds up to the big. Time is your friend.

Did you know that in the midst of each season lies a foretaste of the next? In winter we see the buds of spring developing. In spring we feel the first hints of summer sunshine. The greening of nature. Nature opens up. Until it fully blooms.

At summer's end the nights are already drawing in. There is that first comforting coolness in the night air. The first leaves have browned and lay scattered. The birds swirl in the sky in those formations that say the time has come for change. And the birds just know when that is. The flying ants fly off - wherever they go. The blue of the sky subtly softens.

The first frosts take in late fall/autumn. The wind blows a little cooler. The trees are already near bare. People wear coats. Hats. The earth seems to have gone to sleep - winter is already flirting with that part of the world. Ready to take the reins. *The heat has gone.* And yet in that more gloomy time, there is time for reflection. We often take time to reflect at the end of things, do we not? We look back on what was, and what will never be again: for we and the world are always changing. The same in essence but changes are always occurring. We can't notice them all.

When we plant seeds we may not see them sprout until a certain time has passed. But they do and it does. Wasn't it? Haven't you? You see you can no more stop the snow than you can stop the rain. Or the sun. Or the light at sunset. A new day. At night when we sleep so many changes are possible. The dreaming mind can dream just the right dreams. As all things must change - notice how you can direct that more often in a way that is more to your liking. You may realise that *that old pressure lessens* considerably. For the seasons will change. And who is able to stop the clouds blowing over as they do? Trust your deepest wisdom.

Imagine your new life at some time in the future when you have made all the positive changes you want. How has your life improved? Get the gist of it...From that wonderful future feeling, look back on now, knowing that this is when you changed, aren't you? Haven't you? Wasn't it? That's it.

NOTE WITHOUT EMOTION.

Instead of flying off the handle - what if you pretended for a while to be an objective scientist? Just noticing what was occurring. Taking mental notes. Finding things interesting. Oh, he is doing that, and she is saying this. Why are they doing that? What do they really want?

Even when silly, bad, stupid things happen you could get angry or you could get interested. People are doing X. What is the best response? If you take the future consequences of actions X, Y, and Z into account you'll respond to triggers, stressors, and real crisis with much *greater maturity and calm.*

Although it can <u>seem</u> that the world is ending it isn't. It is changing. But it always is. The change may be limited or radical. Note the change. Find its source. When you can *calmly think things through* things will seem less chaotic, even in the midst of other's chaos. Just because the majority are headless chickens is no reason to run around the barnyard too.

You must protect yourself. There is a time for all emotions. Only do things that are optimally appropriate to that situation. But sometimes the best thing to do is simply note with far less emotion. When you do that and stop acting automatically as you once did you will access your intelligence and humour more often.

Emotions are good when they fulfil the positive purpose for which they exist. You don't need a great big hammer to fix a delicate piece of jewellery. You don't need a gun to play golf. You don't need a sword to spread butter...

Can you recall a time when you remained confident and calm in a sticky situation? How much more flexible and successful were you? If you've done it once the learnings are there and can generalise across into other contexts...*You are in control* of you...

DO ONE THING
AT A TIME.

This was one of the first things I learnt when I was studying hypnosis and stress control. DO ONE THING AT A TIME. One of the main ways we build up background stress is by juggling too many balls at once. Juggling one ball is delightfully, stupidly easy.

If you try to focus on two things you increase the chances of fucking things up. And that will piss you off and then! We're back to square one. We should really be way across the game board by now. A solid, dependable chain of one thing at a time. OVERLOAD = ANGER. It just got too much. You can't do everything at once. Prioritise. Make lists if you must. What is most important now? Do that first, and on and on.

You ever try dating three girls at once? One woman is enough work for anyone. Only take on what is reasonable. Manageable. You will have to *learn to say no*. By saying no you say yes to less stress. Keep that level of energy balanced. Less volcanoes. More gentle ups and downs.

As you aim to do one thing at a time, you'll make less mistakes, you'll feel better, *feel more absorbed*, in control, and satisfied. Leave superman or girl for the comic books. By being comfortably human and knowing that we all have limits you'll help youself in many different ways, that I will never know about. But I promise you, your powers of concentration will increase...

THE HYPER-SENSITIVITY DEFLECTOR!

Most people who are a tad hot tempered TEND to be a bit, shall we say, 'hyper-sensitive'. Perhaps someone was mean to them when they were younger and they have eternally vowed to attack anyone who even...The thing is we do often need feedback from others. It helps to keep our feet on the ground etc.

I know a woman whose mother was so critical of her that she will not listen to any feedback whatsoever because it, 'reminds her of what her mom/mum did.' The problem with this is that we often go through a period during life and learning whereby our old patterns need updating and replacing. If you can't learn from accurate feedback you will not psycho-spiritually grow/mature. You will continue to operate from limited maps which ONLY create further problems. I call these 'robot-loops'.

However, it is possible to 'install' a 'shield' if you like that will stop you crumpling every time you perceive an 'attack'. It will also help if you are genuinely attacked. The best defence is to simply not give a fuck, but for some this is a bridge too far. So with that in mind imagine the following...

Designing the deflector shield.

There is a part that thinks...A part that daydreams...
A part that notices...and a part that notices noticing...
A part that counts...a part that feels, imagines, and dreams...

Just get an idea of a material so strong that nothing can bypass it. It doesn't have to be real. You can make it up. Give it a name worthy of its invulnerable toughness...Okay, when you've done that form it in your mind into some sort of deflector shield: one that could block anything...

Now you have that shield you are going to visualise placing it in your solar plexus area. The little divot at the bottom centre of your chest...

Now this shield stops your power and energy escaping when someone says something to you that you don't like. Instead of that energy leaking out it will be deflected back inside you by the shield. You see it doesn't matter what's going on out there, it does matter what is going on in here.

Imagine seeing a you over there in a situation and someone not very sophisticated says something 'clumsy' or 'careless'. Perhaps they are a primitive communicator...

As you have your deflector shield in place notice that that you does not fold or react. See that energy TRY to escape. An electrical charge ripples around your blocker that zaps that potential energy leak so that it goes back into its place. You keep your energy no matter what is going on around you. Nothing phases you as it once did. That you reacts much more calmly. You have a slight smile on your face. You are wiser and more knowing...

Now go through that process again from your point of view. Through your eyes see that limited person (there are quite a lot of them about) - they emit some words. Which you calmly consider as to their validity.

Feel your deflector leap into action trapping that energy inside of you...Your energy is yours. It is not a thing for others to play with or disturb.

Words are just words: words attempt to describe real experiences. Some people might not have the best of intentions. Some people are weak. Some are dumb. Some are un-nuanced speakers. Some mean well but are verbally clumsy. Whatever. None of this particularly means something.

As most people are quite robotic they often respond automatically. But you are not a robot. You are a fully formed human being who makes choices. You chose the best response. You deserve to feel good, basically happy and confident. From now on you will keep your energy inside. And keep your natural sensitivity: it is an attractive thing.

GOING COLD: AN EXPERIMENT.

Acting exercise: don't feel anything. When I was in Youth Theatre in South London during the 1990s we were taught an acting exercise. We had to sit in a chair and feel nothing. React to nothing. Our faces blank, emotions numb.

A partner, I had a pretty blonde, her job was to provoke me to react. She had to say stuff to me, push me, try to get some response. She couldn't do it. I had spent two years in a weird all boys school. I learnt there how to completely mask all my emotions. She was very impressed. It may have been at this time that she started to develop a crush on me. There can be benefits to controlling your feelings.

Although it might be quite odd try this for 1 minute: go completely 'cold'/unresponsive. Perhaps do it when you have some time on your own. It is possible to consciously shut off feelings. It would be a terrible way to live, but it should show you that you do have the ability to have *control* over *your emotions*.

STOP BEING SO THEATRICAL: MAKE MOLEHILLS OUT OF MOLEHILLS.

All the very angry people I've ever met were drama queens. They habitually overacted. Whether it be shock or fear/panic that outstripped the demands of the situation, whatever. If you think of emotions as having an intensity: 10 being the most intense, 1 the least so. We probably don't need to go all the way to 10 for daily living do we? Maybe a two or three? I dunno. You do.

Do you, had you, up until now, if you were 100% honest with yourself, tended to make mountains out of molehills? It's not a bad thing on the stage. Some people like drama. They like to feel intense emotions. It can be a bit addictive. It can make you *feel more alive.*

What if you felt love more intensely, or calm, or happiness, or sheer bliss, or...? I dunno, you do. What if you started to rate situations with a bit more of a sense of perspective. Nuclear war would be a crap yourself 10. A spilt cup of coffee? Maybe a ½. You can clean it up. No one died. Actually rate things as an experiment. If no one was in d-anger of dying why sweat it?

Over the weeks to come notice if you are objectively overreacting.

If you feel an overreaction coming - slow down, think, find a better way. A sense of humour helps. All solvable problems get solved. Everything we worry about gets solved, sooner or later.

Invent a 'bad-ometer': this rates how bad things really are: zombie-cannibal holocaust 10+. Stubbed toe - painful, very painful. But stress worsens pain. Stop: ask - how bad is this really? My ancestors survived the Ice Age...

IT IS WHAT IT IS.

Many people get angry about things that are. This is normal; many things that are aren't very good. Especially during these odd, destabilised times. However flying into a HULK SMASH! Every time something's not 100% pleasant happens is not the best response is it? What is 'the best response'?

I was at a bus stop. A man saw two cute teenage girls dressed in short dresses and approached them. He obviously asked them why they were wearing such short dresses on such a cold day. It was a chat up line bid. A sad one. One of the girls said, "It is what it is."

It is what it is. It is what it is. There is a great power in that statement. **It is what it is.** It might not be what you want. It most definitely isn't what you like. BUT - IT IS WHAT IT IS! And whatever that less than 100% wonderful situation is, it is reality, and you and they, and everyone is going to have to deal with things as they are. It is what it is...

This should not be interpreted as a blueprint for fatalism. Before you change things you must accept the reality of a situation.

YOU CAN'T EXPECT FROM PEOPLE WHAT THEY CAN'T GIVE.

As certain groups of emotions are linked to expectations you must realise the fact that people can only give what they are capable of giving. People come in all shapes and sizes: stupid - intelligent; or somewhere in between. All dumb people think they're smart because they're too dumb to recognise anything above their abilities. Some smart people are dumb because they imagine that knowledge in one limited field is a sign of 'genius'. The idea that their limited knowledge generalises to all matters that could ever be considered.

Some people cannot love. They are dead on the inside. Some people won't like you. It is what it is. Some people will have 100% wrong and prejudiced views about you. It is what it is. Some people are nasty and mean. Some are indifferent. Some are in a bad mood. You ever try to persuade someone in a bad mood? I nearly always ask people favours when they're smiling. They generally agree because they want to keep that good mood. They are already in a 'yes', agreeable state of mind.

If someone is in a NO! Bad mood - your work will be nudging them toward a good one. You need to break that state; one of the best ways is to get them to physically move or get them to laugh. Laughter breaks down any state: I made a 'depressed' woman burst into laughter. She couldn't stop - despite being 'depressed', apparently. Emotions are stored in bodily poses. If that pose alters the mood will shift. People link places to feelings, states of mind and body. Be aware of this.

You can't expect a tortoise to be a hare. A cat to be rat. Expectations must be grounded in some sort of understanding of the true nature of the beast. If you climb into a lion's cage you can expect to end up as supper.

PEOPLE HAVE THEIR OWN WAY OF DOING THINGS.

It is a truism that it is hard enough to live with people you love, let alone strangers. A lot of anger is inspired by an intolerance of difference. Which is quite funny when you think about it. Some people like tomatoes. Some hate the bastards. Some people hate cucumbers: my brother calls them 'The Devil's Fruit!' I don't mind them at all.

I know someone who knows someone else who only likes tomatoes in burgers. I know someone who won't eat lamb because they feel sorry that 6 month old creatures are eaten. I know other people who think that a six month old sheep, which is fully adult looking, tastes nice with potatoes. What ya gonna do?

I had a hag of a dinner lady/lunch lady when I was little who tried to force me to eat cheese flan which I thought tasted like sick. She said I was spoilt. I knew she was a cunt. I have always been perceptive…

As a teenager I used to go to the school canteen and always ordered a sausage role/puff dog, cheese, and chips (French fries)…One day the lady serving said to me, "You eat the same thing every day! It's not good for you! Blah!" I looked at the twit calmly and smiling replied: "A sausage role…cheese and chips please." I can still smell and taste that now.

Everyone is very different. Even twins are not the same. You can't herd cats. People believe and do weird things. On mass sometimes. Dumb things. Silly things. What ya gonna do? Why get bothered about the fact that the sun is shining? Go get a fan and sit in the shade. You don't like rain? Get an umbrella.

If our energy supply is depleted by wasting it on frivolous trivialities we will waste a whole lot of energy that we could save for truly important things. Just saying...

PEOPLE ARE WHAT THEY ARE.

IS IT WORTH GETTING ANGRY?

Every day we think thousands of individual thoughts. Each of these thoughts affects how we feel - angry thoughts lead to angry emotions. If you think them angrily. If you said, "I am really pissed off!!! in a calm tone you wouldn't get angry.

Now if I hypnotised you formerly those angry thoughts would lessen considerably. I have an idea: I will give you a list of anger-dampening thoughts. What we say repeatedly to ourselves becomes part of our thinking style: should you feel a hulk smash moment arising try the following -

I don't think it's worth getting angry over that.
Hold on, hold on: let me have a think about this first.
Is there a better way to solve this?
Remain calm. Keep your cool.
Ah! My old friend - hold on a moment. I'm not sure if I need you right now.
What's the point in getting angry?
Calm...down. That isn't going to help.
I keep control of where my energy flows.
I need to stop acting automatically. THINK!
I am more flexible and creative when I stay calm.
I'm tired. When I get tired my temper used to flare. Calm down, Calm down.
There's no point making a scene. I will get what I want by remaining

calm.
Nothing is to be gained by getting angry - calm down.
I need to relax my face, hands, neck – when I used to get angry the stress starts there and spreads. Chill out. Let it go.
I am feeling much better and getting on with people in much better ways. Things are working. Don't ruin it with that old response.
I'm not a little kid: no more temper tantrums.
No. I don't do that any more.
It's better to be calm.
Although I am entitled to get angry If I do I would be giving away my power.
That would be unhelpful right now...
Oh no! Not you again! Fuck off I'm having fun!

Get the idea? Make up your own. You are what you think. Think differently: get different results. Most of the time it simply isn't worth getting angry is it? Catch anger early. ***When any emotion is at its weakest it is easiest to stop.***

ANGER FOLLOWING MANIPULATION.

No one likes to be conned. To be taken for a ride. However, being manipulated is a fairly regular experience for many people. On a daily basis. The amount of cons people fall for is staggering; this is part of the reason that I wrote my **How to Manipulate Everyone** series.

When you realise someone lied and took advantage of you, you are more than entitled to get angry. With one caveat: what good will it do now? If you noticed the con and got angry beforehand that would be of some use.

What's the best response? Instead of getting angry you could take direct action to ensure that that person or persons cannot con anyone else again. You could write a letter to a superior of that person. You could start a political campaign or pressure group to bring about change. You can take legal action against them. If that's possible.

The point is people should face some form of rational retribution for wrongdoing. Sometimes getting angry is 100% the right response for dealing with the whole host of con men and women out there. And there are many.

You have learned that not all people should be trusted. You won't be so naive next time will you? If it sounds too good to be true it probably is. Psychopaths will tell you what you want to hear.

Instead of looking back and angrily regretting here's a tip: don't fall for any more cons. Trust me - you'll be far less angry. Yes, there is sucker born every minute. Don't let that sucker be you.

Connected to this: beware of any politician who stokes anger. Politicians should responsibly persuade by presenting facts. If they don't do that - if they go for an emotive response, they are manipulating you. Wise up.

ANGER FROM INCOMPETENCE.

One of the religions in Britain is the worshipping of the National Health Service (NHS be thy name!). Like a deity it is beyond criticism. The masses are completely irrational towards its true nature. Nurses and doctors are treated as though they are 'heroes', unlike real heroes they actually believe they are. Now let's tell the truth...

I had a client come to see me whose father had been terribly treated by NHS staff. His treatment was shoddy and incompetent. After he died as a result of this tenth- rate treatment she felt permanently angry. I saw her and hypnotised it away you might say.

I saw an old man whose wife had been butchered by an NHS doctor. She had gone in for a minor operation, but the incompetent moron that operated on her had somehow damaged her spine. She could not walk thereafter. This couple had looked forward to retirement. The man had looked after disabled children his whole life. Now his wife was disabled due to negligence. He was not a happy bunny.

Another lady I saw had had incompetent NHS doctors bungle surgery after she gave birth. This led to constant, misery-inducing pain. She was a young woman with a lively little boy. She couldn't play with him. Merely going to the toilet was an agonising experience. Despite what had happened she would not take legal action against the Holy of Holies - the NHS.

Now, I am not just picking on medical incompetence. Although frankly, why shouldn't I? As any society becomes increasingly less meritocratic incompetence and failure becomes the norm, and it becomes normalised.

You must hold incompetent people responsible for their actions: I don't care if it's the Queen of Sheba. People who harm others due to their incompetence must be punished and prevented from harming anyone else. You do know, for example, that sizeable amounts of would-be 'professionals' cheat on their exams.

I don't want you to end up like the poor people I've mentioned. Do not worship anything human. Hold incompetent people accountable. You can't go around hitting people but you can hit them in the wallet.

Revenge has a very bad wrap. Sometimes a form of 'revenge' is called for. Albeit in a civilised format. There is still such a thing as justice, and a just 'war'.

THE BLAME GAME!

This may seem to contradict the last topic. But when we get angry we often instinctively blame others. It kinda comes with anger as an added bonus. This natural response often makes matters far worse. Often we are the cause of the thing that made us angry and we have to admit that. You fucked up. It happens. Don't take that out on someone else. People who overdo angry have a bad habit of poisoning nearest and dearest relationships. Who is most likely to be with you when you, as we say in England, 'lose your rag'? Family and friends, daily co-workers.

Let me tell you a story: two little boys were playing in a playground. As they played one got overexcited and fell over and hurt himself. He was embarrassed and told his friend off! In steps his mum/mom: "Don't you blame so and so because you fell over!" she told him. Ah, the swift and arbitrary justice of mothers.

If you get angry stop looking for other people to blame and take your foul mood out on. Ask, if you must, "Hold on. Before I lash out - am I to blame?"

Extreme anger should never be directed toward children. It utterly terrifies them. A raging adult looks like a murdering ogre to a little child. And they are too little to fight back. Children do naughty things. It shows spirit. Explaining why something is naughty or bad is far better than going nuclear. Good children sometimes do naughty things.

I don't want to tell anyone how to raise their kids but that 'naughty step' stuff is moronic. It was developed in the late 60s. Hardly a time of great common sense.

You must be rational when it comes to apportioning blame. Starting a nuclear war is off the charts bad. Accidentally breaking a plate is a bit of a pain, but not the end of the world. Formerly angry people need to *get things in their proper perspective*. Anger does distort our perceptions.

Alcohol and anger.

We may as deal with this here. Anger and alcohol misuse are linked. I know this from therapy sessions I have carried out. If anger and booze are best friends for you, cut down on your drinking. Booze befuddles brains and lowers your inhibitions making anger outbursts more likely. No one is at there best during a hangover are they? If you want to be more chilled remove any potential anger triggers.

A CRISIS OF 'FAITH'.

Anger may have or might become an issue with you if you face what can only be termed a 'crisis of faith'. This is in no way a religious issue. It is deeply spiritual.

All human beings have a 'philosophy', a kinda semi-conscious guidebook for living. It is based on what others told you about X, Y, and Z, and on what you have personally experienced. NLP calls this your 'map'; although map theories predate NLP. See my **Force of Suggestion** series.

Crisis of faith occur when you 'operate' from an unrealistic map. The feedback you get from reality does not get you the results you want. You get frustrated and angry. Which is understandable but pointless because it will solve NOTHING!

Anger is often a signal that your map is not fully realistic. Whose is? No one knows everything about reality. For example some people actually believe that if they are better than others at a job/skill etc. they will get that job promotion etc. Oh dear. When they don't get it they get angry. Excellence in any field, as things currently stand in West World, is no criteria for advancement.

If I work hard and play by the 'rules'; oh dear. As you grow and mature you will have many moments where you realise that you have been living in a fairy tale. Good and bad people filled your head with nonsense.

Unfortunately in order to have a realistic, non-anger inducing philosophy you must accept reality as it is. You don't have to like it.

Remember social reality is real, but it can be altered. All the social realities that have ever existed have a life cycle. Things like gravity don't. But ideas come and go. Ideas come and go...

Success occurs when you know what social reality is and work ways around it. A philosophy for living should be permanently updated and worked upon as you interact with reality - be willing to ditch those fantasies **_when you come up against a brick wall; don't get angry - think: AH! An opportunity to improve my map._** Chill. Get curious to _learn_ more and more and more.

FIND YOURSELF: FIND YOUR MISSION.

Many people lack 'direction'. What do I mean by that? I will give you an example. 1,692. If you reach the age of 78 the average US citizen has been guesstimated to watch 1,692 hours of TV per week. This adds up to a chilling 15 years of your life totally wasted. No wonder so many people are angry. 31% of US households own 4 or more TVs. Many have 1 per room. 88% of US citizens watch TV in the evening to 'unwind'. There is nothing whatsoever relaxing about TV. By the time a US high school student graduates they have watched over 200, 000 acts of violence on TV. Children's cartoons show 20 acts of violence per hour. Source: **Credit Donkey** website. **Television Statistics: 23 mind-numbing Facts to Watch.**

Question: is one of the major purposes of your life to watch TV? Is 15 years wasted life time a good use of your precious life? In that time what have you actually accomplished that is meaningful?

Now I picked on TV because it is an easy target. Sure I watch some TV now and then, who doesn't? Everyone likes watching a good movie: not that there are many these days, but...15 FUCKING YEARS!! Staggering when you think about it.

People who waste their life really shouldn't moan about being frustrated. In that time you could learn a multitude of skills. You could achieve an untold number of goals. In 15 spare years - what couldn't you do? If you are a TV addict, and yes TV addiction is very real (15 YEARS!), perhaps you had better find your life's purpose.

You are here for a reason. I don't know what that is: you do. The deepest core of who you are knows why you are here. It has probably been trying to tell you, but up to now you haven't listened. "I have no time to exercise." "I would like to learn piano but I have no time." "I would like to..."15 years.

Imagine you had only 2 years to live: if that is all the time you had left - where would you go? What would you really want to do? What would you really want to learn? What experiences would you really like to have? Who or what type of people do you want to spend your time with?

You can have an extra 15 years of meaningful experience, or you can piss it all down the drain. The choice is yours.

WHEN YOU SHOULD GIVE SOMEONE A BOLLOCKING!

You are entitled to protect yourself from attack. You are entitled at times to give someone a good verbal dressing down. You are entitled to get righteously angry when appropriate. You must set boundaries with regards to behaviour that you will accept from others. Your red lines. I don't know you. You know you. Take some time now to specifically set your red lines. When should you get angry? When is is precisely right to do so? I leave this task to you.

TIME TO UNWIND.

If anger has been a problem you need to take some time to unwind. You need to *lower your overall level of background stress*. Do you take the time to chill out often enough? If you are wound too tight something will snap.

I want you to realistically assess where and when, and probably more importantly, with whom your life is most stressful. ***The best way to reduce stress is to eliminate actual stress triggers from you life.*** Can you avoid that person? See them less often? Cut them out entirely if necessary?

Can you retrain and leave that job? Of course you can. Sometimes change needs a calm mind. A bit of honest self-reflection and a bit of courage. You need that courageous moment or decision, and after that you never look back. You have to do what has to be done.

If you *commit to a change* it can make the interim period better. You know that you are moving toward something preferable. That can make you *feel better.* Every day is a closer step toward what you actually want. Most people sell themselves short. If you expect too little you will be very glad to know that that is very easy to achieve. But there is a great price. A lifetime of misery.

We were supposed to be talking about unwinding. Do you take time to do relaxing things? To have fun? How often? For how long? Are you a workaholic who NEVER takes breaks? You need work breaks: 15/20 minutes during the mid morning and mid afternoon. At least an hour for lunch. Workers fought hard to have the human right to have a well-earned rest.

When you get sufficient rest you can recover. Your stress levels go down. Your ability to concentrate improves. Your head clears. You feel far less frazzled. Rest is needed to keep sensory overload at bay. Sufficient rest = superior productivity. You will make far fewer mistakes and so get more done. You are human. Most people develop 'stress-related' problems because they stop acting human which is quite silly. A cat never stops acting like a cat. A dog barks and cocks its leg to take a piss.

Why is it that humans, of all the animals, with their 'superior' brains are the only living organisms that 1. Doesn't want to act like a human? Follow their nature. 2. Don't think they be adverse consequences from not acting like a human?

It takes a real good dose of brainwashing to lose your human nature. Get in touch with your needs, listen to the messages from your body, images that pop into your head, feelings, instincts, intuitions, your conscience. The so-called 'system' tells you to refuse to listen to your 'instincts' even though that is the deep you. Why would anyone tell you to stop paying attention to yourself?

ANGER AND CONTROL.

One of the main things to recognise is the role of 'control' and anger events. Basically anger events are caused by a rising feeling of an immediate, past, or future lack of control. Why is control so important to human existence? It's not rocket science: the greater the degree of control you have the more likely you are to survive.

Let's take our supposed 'cave man' ancestors. A naked adult human is not a great threat to anyone as he or she stands. They are surrounded by the so-called Pleistocene mega-fauna. These giant hairy beasts could probably kill you by taking a great big shit on your head. They are not scared of the humans. But...

Mankind can organise. Small as he seems in comparison to mega-beasts he has a large, creative brain. He is the most adaptable species on the planet, able to survive in any environment. He simply changes the way he lives. His strength and weakness is that he adapts to everything. This capacity for meta-adaptation helps him survive.

He has control over his environment. The animals do change the environment, but not in a planed, schematic way. Man has his brain and his hands. These allow him to make tools. He masters the secret of fire-making. This allow him to stay warm at night and during the winter months. He can ward off large, possible predatory animals who are scared of fire. He can hunt the animals in gangs and use cunning and strategy to outwit them: then he cooks them on his fire.

He develops tools to further control his environment. Cutting flints. Stone-headed spears and arrows. He discovers clay and makes pots. He notices that he can grow and control some of the vegetation he likes around him. He breeds particular strains of crops. Eventually he decides to herd some of the animals in a controlled way. He pens them into certain grazing lands using fences/hedges. This is much more efficient. It saves him time and energy. He only breeds the most docile animals; they are thus more controllable. You could go on...

In a way Stone Age man was much freer than us. He is much more the master of his own fate. He doesn't pay taxes. He has no powerful gang forcing him to do that which he doesn't want to. That system of herding humans by other 'humans' doesn't start till the end of the Ice Age.

Now the system controls you. You have to get up at certain times. Obey orders from a slave driver. You have to work to make someone else wealthy. To be honest you were better off with flint and fire in many ways!

Now in the 'modern world' we have a large series of forces from rich and powerful people untroubled by conscience who want to take all the power away from the 'masses'. The masses fought for hundreds of years to get some power and control back from 'them'.

A person with 0% control over their life is a slave. You are not a slave. You are free. No matter what any system tells you what its relation to you is: you are free. The question is how much freedom do you want? How are you going to get that freedom? What has to change to make you have the maximum freedom possible? With freedom comes control. The powerful have always done their utmost to jealously preserve what they call 'freedom' for themselves. The freedom to do as THEY want and the freedom to control YOU. The question is: are you going to let anyone control you?

Man was meant to be free and independent. Any 'system' that does not reflect this psycho-spiritual reality is evil. Evil is defined, at least on one level, as organised control-freakery. There has never, will never be, a despotic system that protects your freedoms: they spend all their time taking the masses' former freedoms away.

Now, as you are a free man or woman you must realise now that your human heritage is the ability to control your environment. In any situation you will have a degree of control. Others have their own wants, you'll have to negotiate and compromise at times. What I have been long-windedly trying to say is that:

THE MORE CONTROL YOU TAKE OVER YOUR LIFE THE LESS ANGRY YOU'LL BE.

Anger is in fact not possible when YOU have the control. It's time to take back control? Where will you start?

DID YOU LACK LOVE?: LOVE ALLOWS CONTROL.

There is evidence that it is a lack of love in our life that leads to anger attacks. I mean the word 'love' in the widest possible; sense. Let's say you lost your job for no fault of your own, or the government shut down your small business that it took you 10 years to create for a whole 2 years based on, ahem, 'reasons', and unsurprisingly can trace your 'anger issues' to this event etc.

Now someone making you lose a job or business is not a loving act. It does not fill you with a sense of feeling appreciated or respected. Thrown to the wolves you might say.

People feel anger when they embark on a career path in which they cannot advance, no matter how good at the job they are. This may be caused by corruption, social prejudice, racial prejudice - whatever. None of which are loving acts.

You may have been dumped from a relationship you imagined was going great: he or she was 'the one', except they weren't, and you aren't getting any younger, and...People break up, it happens, but a source of love and appreciation is now demonstrably gone and my wise-ass/arse comments don't help...

Look, it seems that humans need to be loved, appreciated, respected, and deserve a fair chance. Who knew!?? If you have suffered an 'anti-love' event may I suggest the following: get back out there and get some lovin'. Love soothes anger better than anything else.

Rebuild that business - this time take measures to make that fucker bulletproof. Get another lover. Find an audience that appreciates you in another venue. Never let anyone's prejudice hold you back from shining. There are ALWAYS other ways. Get a load of big, fat juicy love in your life and feel far less stressed. Don't take pills for fuck's sake. Get more love!

AVOID STRESS, AVOID ANGER.

There is a great way to avoid getting angry: avoid stressful situations as much as you can. Some people are inherently more stressful to be around than others. Some people are too noisy. Some people are inconsiderate. Some are rude. Some are condescending. Some are outrageously, painfully dumb. Some people only want to talk about themselves. People who don't listen. Know it alls. Some people endlessly boast etc., etc., etc.. Why would you want to be around human stress triggers like that?

Spending money you can't afford to is stress-inducing. Shopping at peak hours can be very stressful. Some areas are more dangerous than others and should be avoided. Taking on too much. Doing things you don't want to do to just to make someone else happy. Why don't they want to make you happy?

You know I stopped going to any bar or nightclub that has bouncers ages ago. You know why? 1. I don't like bouncers - they're loser dicks. 2. Any place that needs bouncers has fights there quite regularly. Who in their right mind wants to be around low IQ morons who enjoy starting fights with random strangers?

Putting things off instead of facing up to them. Ignoring the truth that boldly stares you in the face. Making decisions based on bad information from unreliable sources. Many people like to make life tougher than it already is. As life is tough enough for most people I leave you with this advise: ***try to minimise stress by avoiding obviously misery-inducing situations.*** You might need to take time to think about it. Is it worth the stress? Really? Cut out the stress, cut out anger. None of this is rocket science. Common sense is by far the best 'therapy'.

CONCLUSIONS ON ANGER CONTROL.

Anger is the human howl of pain. A pain caused by frustration at all the shit we have to put up with in life. I get it. Things aren't the way you want them to be. On many occasions anger may be fully justified. However, that does not mean it is the best or optimum response. It may not be best for your health and the health of intimate relationships. It may be dangerous to unleash a rage attack on a stranger. These are weird and fucked-up times. You don't want to hurt someone, or get hurt, or end up in jail/ prison. It's not worth it. Have you ever seen those girls with those men? The men start facing off, exchanging heated words, and...a girl steps in and says "He's not worth it... (insert name here!)" And the lady is right. 99% of the time anger is not worth the effort it demands.

Prolonged stress from anger causes skin problems, weakens your immune system, can cause a heart attack or stroke if you're not in tip-top shape, is linked to anxiety and its crazy cousin 'depression'. Or as I call it natural response to loss and unmet needs. High blood pressure. Sleepless nights. Anger can create inflammation in your airways and reduce your lung capacity.

Some quack therapists say 'focus on the present' blah, bah to stop anger. No focus on the future and how much shittier your life will be if you keep acting like Captain Rage Turd. There is so much twee, STOOPID advise out there on 'anger management'. Try breathing deep breaths. Take 'time out' to calm down. Oh God! It's enough to make you angry.

Let me leave you with some words: words are very useful if they are actually helpful...There follows a somewhat hypnotic story called - Captain Rage Turd!

THE STORY OF CAPTAIN RAGE TURD.

Captain Rage Turd was a superhero. He could fly and all that shit. Jump over buildings. Turn himself invisible so he could scratch his arse/ass in public. But his main 'ability', if you could call it that, was to go from completely calm and happy to 100% rage in 1 second. One minute he'd be talking away like a regular human being then - POW! THWACK! His head turned bright red, grew 3 feet in diameter, and veins popped out on his 21 inch, macho-man neck. He barked out words like a fucking crazy, psycho dog straining on a leash. Anything could set him off. He was a touchy fucker.

One day his friend Shatman who had the power to crap himself every 5 minutes farted. It was quite the fart. He'd been eating beans and eggs - you can imagine the results. Captain Rage Turd's fancy new carpet was ruined. The Captain exploded going hyper-fucking ballistic! Expletives hurled through the air, striking Shatman and pinning him to the wall. This only made him crap himself again. "Why isn't EVERYTHING perfect!" cried out Captain Rage Turd. "If EVERYTHING was perfect I'd NEVER be angry again!!!"

Shatman cowered in the corner. Straining to hold in his biggest crap yet. Captain Rage Turd had been angry before. But nothing like this. He was smashing up every item in his near perfect house. Flying through walls with his fists punching destructively!

Someone might get hurt.

As luck would have it Lady Rocket Knockers lived in the apartment below. Although one of the Team of Legends super-heroines she liked to practise violin in between fighting crime and doing social work. The noise in the room above alerted her dick-head sense that something was terribly amiss....

TO BE CONTINUED...

Now, I hear you had some problems with regards to a certain emotion. Emotions are funny things. Words ride them like boats on the sea...your best armour in life is your unswerving faith in yourself and your sense of humour. Getting active with a regular exercise routine of your choosing will work wonders. Fresh, country air from time to time. Getting things in their proper perspective. Knowing that each and both of you know how to control stress levels. Continuing to make wise decisions based on good information. Taking responsibility to change your life, to mould and direct it. Being tolerant of difference. Appreciating the deep value of those you love and care for. Looking out for opportunities no matter how things change. Knowing that you have more control than you thought. Thinking for yourself. Always learning. Being much more patient. Taking on just the right amount of whatever: having enough time. Doing more of what you enjoy.

At a deep level, whilst you sleep perhaps, and dream a dream of change, you will be pleasantly delighted to learn than a number of specific and appropriate changes can and do occur. Which will you notice first? Which ones do others point out to you? The unconscious mind can make these changes for you, and you need not know, consciously, how any of this positive, new direction occurred. No matter what happens know this: if you act wisely...all is well...

TRANSMISSION RESUMES...

Lady Rocket Knockers knocked open Captain Rage Turd's front door with her unfeasibly large tits. Both Shatman and Captain Rage Turd stood there dumbfounded! The blonde super goddess stood there bathed in golden sunlight. Her spandex outfit glistening. Perplexed, Captain Rage Turd was about to explode when Lady Rocket Knockers strode toward him using the power of feminism. With one shake of her super shoulders she knocked Captain Rage Turd Clean out with her super knockers....

In his state of unconsciousness the super hero began to dream. In that dream he found himself on a desert island somewhere in the middle of nowhere. Where is the middle of nowhere? Wherever it was it was so calm there. He sat on the beach in just his underpants. Usually he wore them on the outside of his super-outfits. It was a good thing he wiped his bottom properly.

There on the beach, in the middle of nowhere he noticed all the natural beauty around him. The natural stillness or rhythms of nature filled him with an amazing sense of deep refreshment.

He could feel the soft, light-brown sand massaging his feet as he walked. Here, inside this place, all was well in the world. This sense of calm spread all the way through his body, as if by magic...As he calmed all the way down he noticed that everything looked more real. All his senses came alive. His head was clear. His body relaxed. He noticed his feet were very relaxed. His shins were comfy. He knees rested. His thighs just took it easy as he sat down and noticed the waves. They seemed to hypnotise him with their unending, natural rhythms.

That feeling of peace spread up to his waist. It filled his tummy. He noticed his breathing. As he did it changed. As it changed he took a deep breath and lay down looking at the blue sky, which was slowly turning to sunset. His back muscles seemed to sink into the sand. His arms were free of all past tension. His hands felt rested for the first time in ages. His neck let go. His facial muscles felt as if a highly trained expert had magically massaged all that former tension away.

As he lay there, feeling comfort from head to toe, he noticed the sun set. The purple-orange clouds soothed his vision. The sky was a magical gradient of soft peach to soft, pale, horizon blue. He simply gazed and felt whole again. The first stars appeared. Twinkling. One, two, three. He could see the connections of constellations. Looking at the majesty of the universe like that made him naturally reflect on so many differing things that he began to daydream. Some kind of healing was occurring.

The sky turned a tranquil shade of dark blue. It reminded him of velvet. As he lay there, aware of this or that, as his attention shifted pleasantly, he noticed that he was noticing a thought that said. "Get up, pleasantly, and take a swim" And so he did.

As a superhero he had no fears of sharks or sea monsters. He could hold his breath for hours safely, but he could also breathe perfectly well in any element. So he simply walked under water slowly and took a look at the sea floor.

All was empty. Not a fish in sight. And so he swam. His body felt strong and 100% refreshed. He swam deeper and deeper into the ocean. All the way down he went.

After some time he chanced to spy a shipwreck. He made for it. He swam between the holes in the barnacled beams. Whales sang in the far distance. This sound soothed him. And then he saw it! A treasure chest!

Using his super strength he pried the object open. Inside was treasure beyond your wildest possible dreams. But he scooped that aside because he knew that in the core was a greater treasure. A treasure beyond measure. And there it was. An old parchment. Somehow unmolested by the sea. He unfurled it. At the top of the document he read the words: 'The Secret of Secrets!'

The secret was only for him, as this process is only for you...I do not know what he read. Only he knew. He paused and began to ponder...many answers to problems emerged...He had a moment of utter clarity and realisation about so many differing things. Whatever those things were he knew that when he returned to the surface it would be as the person he really was. And that made him feel glad.

At that point he heard the voice of what he believed to be a beautiful mermaid. So pretty it sounded, like the tinkling of silver bells. And so he awoke in the arms of Lady Rocket Knockers. She stroked his hair comfortingly. "I think you knocked some sense into me..." he said calmly, and then, in that way they do in superhero tale endings, first he, then she, and of course Shatman began to laugh...

Printed in Great Britain
by Amazon

41562124R00059